Write letters of your soul.
  Charlynne xx

Letters to my soul
By Charlynne Bryan

Letters to my soul

Copyright 2019 © by Charlynne Bryan

This book is copyright under the Berne convention and as such no reproduction of this book should be made without the permission of the author. If you share poems from this book on social media, please credit the author.

Instagram: @mizz_b_ryan
Twitter: @cookieb20

Charlynne Bryan

To *You*

The dreamer of dreams
The actor of actions
The believer of beliefs
The creator of creativity
To you for being curious
For being open
For being receptive
For being you

Letters to my soul

About the author

Charlynne Bryan crafts words into stories. Inspired by the life of the many people she has encountered along the way; she is a poet who incorporates her life stories and the stories of others into her craft and fashions them into works of art. She has performed poetry at various venues, facilitated poetry sessions with adults and children, incorporated her words in artistic gifts and conducted poetry workshops aimed at allowing people to share stories through poetry. Charlynne is exceptionally gifted in performance poetry and inspires people to channel their voice so their message can be heard.

Charlynne Bryan

Fall back

Letters to my soul

Charlynne Bryan

I am hurting
Yearning
Longing
Healing
Being the best that I can be
In this space that I am
Doing the best that I can do
With the opportunities that
I've been given
Taking it one day at a time
One step at a time
One minute at a time
I move forward
Advance
Elevate
Aspire
I connect to love
To mother earth
To father God
I remember
I am human
I am spirit
I am free
Free to be me
Whoever I am
Whoever I am meant to be

Letters to my soul

Believe what you like
About whatever
You will
But know
That whatever you believe
Will be proven
True

Perception is the difference
Between right and wrong

Charlynne Bryan

Letters to my soul

It's been the hardest
To learn
- This lesson
That sometimes,
The people you love
Don't love you back.

Charlynne Bryan

Every now and then I like
To eat ice cream
And think of you
I use the ice cream
To numb the pain
Of having you gone
And I use the thoughts
To remind me
That you
Were
Never
Good for me

Letters to my soul

They will come.
With petals shooting
Out of their mouths
With honey flowing from
Their tongue
With galaxies you've
Never seen before
Lighting up their eyes
They will tell you
All the things you wish
You could whisper to yourself
All the dreams you have yet to chase
All the sands they have counted
With you in a future you cannot yet see
And they will hold you
So tight
That you cannot see their petals rot
Their honey crystalise
Their galaxies dim
They will kiss your eyes shut
And your ears close
So you remain unable to hear
The lies beneath their talk
And if you continue to believe them
Before long
They will take your self
And replace it with something

Charlynne Bryan

You no longer recognise
But remember
Always remember
That even losing yourself
Is not the end
If you can still breathe and
Remember, just remember
That you've made it through
Their hurricane
So their quiet storm
Has nothing on you

Letters to my soul

I remember days when
I could touch your sunshine
And not turn to dust
Now it feels like
I am reconstructing myself
Out of the ashes left over
From your singeing embrace
Trying to quell the burn
Trying to become again
                    -Phoenix by force

Charlynne Bryan

You are greatness
Waiting to explode

Letters to my soul

And they know it
When they look at us
They can see it
Yes they hear it
Even before we can say it
And they fear it
This silent determination
That keeps us going
This unfettered resolve
And it scares them
Because we will not
Give up and we will
Not give in

Charlynne Bryan

If you love yourself
Truly love you
It wouldn't matter
If they didn't

Letters to my soul

Let's sit here and be
Silent together
There is no need for words
I can feel what your
Heart is saying through
The words you do not speak

Charlynne Bryan

PRIVILEGE

When he knocks at your door
Before he asks, answer him
Tell him you know
That you are beautiful beyond belief
Tell him you know
That you are so special
That the stars
Stop and stare at you
Tell him you know
That your confidence scares
Everyone who sees it
And that you know he is
More afraid than anyone else
Before he tries to tell you
Tell him that you
Have tasted love in its purest from
That you are not broken
Or need fixing
Tell him that you are complete
Let him know that
You do not need him
To love you for you to be free
Let him know that you are enough
Tell him it is your pleasure
To have him there but

Letters to my soul

Remind him how privileged he is
That you even opened the door

Charlynne Bryan

We keep isolating bits of ourselves
Instead of looking at the whole person
As though focusing on one
Attribute
Will make us whole again

Letters to my soul

What if
You are already
The salvation you need?
What if you already are
Your own prince charming?

Charlynne Bryan

Little things
Whisper loudly
Knock about my head
Dance in my stomach
Little things
Hide in plain sight
Walk the tightrope
Pop out of the box
Bounce around
Push against my boundaries
Create their own
Little things drive me crazy
Keep me guessing
Never really knowing
Little things stand up to me
Hold me down
Keeps me thinking
Keeps me sane

Letters to my soul

3 3 9 A

His eyes were evening walks
At art galleries. They were
Moonlight dances under the stars,
Deep conversations at twilight and dinner
Crossed legged on the floor. His eyes were
Morning messages of good wishes,
Checking in at odd times...
Asking if I'd eaten. His eyes
Were the opening conversation
Before every new movie and after
Every old song.

Charlynne Bryan

She whispered sweet poetry in her stories
Like nectar to my soul and
Soon I began to see myself reflected in her eyes
I knew her words could heal
Because those were words to make
The body inside my body less invisible
And as she said them
My layers peeled themselves off
And ran back into
The dark corners they had crawled out of

Letters to my soul

PARROTTE

Do I squawk loudly and flap about aimlessly to you?
Do you think I am too loud for my own good?
And too bright to fit into your mould?
I am a bird of paradise
Colourful and vibrant
Social and flamboyant
Strong in my opinions and mannerism
You may not like that I talk too much
But yes, I am a Parrotte and I will
Speak, I will stand out
I will fly

Charlynne Bryan

I see you looking at me
Into me
Peeling back the layers
Undressing me with your eyes
Staring into my soul
Even when my head is turned away
And my eyes are closed
It's clear you want me
On your tongue
It's clear you miss me
In your bed
Like the drug you're quitting
Why deny that I am your aphrodisiac?
Why starve yourself of the pleasure
I can erupt in you?

Letters to my soul

I waited for you
Eyes peeled and focused
On the door you walked
Out of asking me to wait for you
To stand by
Until you returned
Days turned to nights
Months turned to years
My heart grew weary
My eyes grew heavy
Tears no longer fall
I am no longer waiting
You lost that hope when
You refused to look back
As you said you would

Charlynne Bryan

GODDESS

I'm every woman
Sister to all girls wishing
Peace was their daily bread
Mother to every orphan
Affected by war
Famine and disease
I am every daughter
Standing on the front line
Every girl waiting for her time
I am every hope
Every dream
I am every ordinary
Female who realises her inner queen
I am her whisper
From the side lines
Building up to power
I am her…

Letters to my soul

UNLABELLING

Call me woman
Place your labels upon me
So you can keep me in my place
Wrap tendrils of my spirit around your
Fingers and lace flowers through my hair
As you call me beautiful
Let the fragrance of your words hold me captive
Sweet nothings dripping off your tongue
Reminding me that it was you who named me
Call me feminine, curves made to appease you
As I labour in vain... hands made to comfort you
As I suffer in pain. lips made to savour you
As I call out your name
Call me rib
Taken from your side to help you serve
Fused into the backbone that must now hold you
Yet left behind you
Call me property, bounty traded by
Fathers to bring honour
Treasure hidden by mothers to save honour
Honour taken by brothers to save face
Call me captive
Slave to the labels you've placed upon me
Driven by the will to just let be
Fighting a war others refuse to name

Charlynne Bryan

Call me sacred
Body full of purpose
Driven to want choices
Willing to claim nothing unless I say
Call me... call me
Call me nothing
        unless
            I
                choose.

Letters to my soul

SACRIFICIAL LAMB

How did this body, this temple
Become so sullied by bad intentions?
When did this body become the offering
Laid down preceding supplication for forgiveness
Instead of the altar
Where offerings are given?
How did this body become destined to be
The burnt offering
Paid as penance to the gods
Instead of the place where penance is paid?

Charlynne Bryan

REINVENT YOURSELF

They told me to reinvent myself
As though the me that I am was somehow
Fraudulent
As if by some magic chant I could cease to be
This
Reinvent, as though something
Was wrong with the original
As though stepping forward
And casting off this shell
Ahanged the core of my identity
As though it wasn't ok to be me
As I am
In this space
Holding this existence in my being
How preposterous to think
That I would agree
That being the current me was undesirable
How absurd a notion that I was flawed
Lacking
Incomplete
And I see: have I not been the me that I
Have always wanted?
The me that I've been waiting for?
Why reinvent perfection?
New year: Same me!

Letters to my soul

DUST

Been fallin' to pieces
Breaking off of myself
Turning to ash
When the dust settles
Who will I be?
Remnant of a vision
I used to be:
Apparition or
Transformation?

Charlynne Bryan

I AM THE POEM

I try to slap words onto paper
String metaphor after metaphor
Begging for sense
Force my words to dance a pirouette
And shimmy down to my fingertips onto
The page
Missing the link
Until I realise

I am the poem
The burst of angry spilling from lips
The bubble of excitement beneath the surface of
Skin
A million words twisted into power
That is me

I am the poem
The dash of sexy undertones under bedsheets
The subtle innuendos between spoonfuls of chaste
Speech
The winky emojis, the LOLs
That is me

I am the poem
The message standing on the outside of the line

Letters to my soul

The lewd, shrill responses skirting the confines
The protest barricading the sidewalks of time
I am the voice
That is me.

Charlynne Bryan

EYE OF THE BEHOLDER

What if I told you that when I looked at me,
I didn't see beautiful?
Would you try to reassure me that the sun
That shines in my eyes burns with the
Intensity of a thousand suns?
Would you try to convince me that my skin
sparkles like diamonds and gleams in the light?
Would you call me silly and ask if I couldn't see
What the mirror tried to scream every time
I peered in?
And would you think it odd when I chose to
Look away instead of trying to see what
You stare into when you look at my face?
What if I told you that I don't see beautiful
What I see is me?
What if I said instead that when I peer
Into the glass
I look at the depths of my heart
Bursting through my smile
And the truth of my character shining
From my eyes
Because you see I don't need your reassurance
I need you to understand that your
Concept of beauty is fleeting,
Ever changing and irrelevant to me.

Letters to my soul

HERO

You can do it you know
Take to the sky on broken wings
And still muster the power to soar
Higher than your dreams could ever carry you
You can ride above the myth of doubt
And create the legend that slays the dragons
And the type of charming that saves the
Damsel in distress...
You can be heroic even when fear gnaws at
Your feet and anxious claws at your chest
Even when the maze of emotions
Threaten to keep you lost
You can do it you know...
Weave a yarn in and out of despair
Dance on empty promises and turn them
Into musical masterpieces
And be more, way more than just what you
Were told you could be.

Charlynne Bryan

AND THEY LIVED HAPPILY EVER AFTER

I learnt
That there is no 'the one'
That prince charming never comes
That standing in the tower
Waiting for salvation is a mistake I can't
Afford to make - again
I learnt
That sometimes, poisoned apples are the way
Out
That ugly stepsisters and dragons are
Just distractions not hindrances
That the breadcrumbs that lead to the
Forest are the same breadcrumbs that lead to
The witches house
That the wolf has been judged harshly
Because he let his desire be known
But ain't no one pointing fingers at the
Beast just 'cause he was cursed...
As though that's an excuse for bad
Behaviour.
I learnt
That fairy tales don't exist in the way we
Want them to
That nothing is ever black and white

Letters to my soul

And the truth, the truth is always hidden
Somewhere between the shades of grey.

Charlynne Bryan

U P R S I N G

The voice that laid dormant is now awake
No longer silent.
And being woken from slumber,
This voice roars above the din and rush
Of waterfalls
Above the gentle melodies of blue
Summer skies
This voice pierces through beautiful rose
Tinted facades
And shatters glass ceilings created to keep
Growth from occurring
This voice booms around empty spaces and
Permeates every corner
This voice initiates a revolution
Calls to a nation
Demands attention
The voice that once said nothing
Is letting it all out!

Letters to my soul

INTERROGATION

There are some questions that we never ask up front
Like will you value my faith in God the way
You say you want to value my p***y
Will you stand with me and be silent while
I offer myself up in prayer and ask for
Forgiveness from the sins that haunt me?
Or will you just want to f**k me?
Will you put aside your human desires and court me
And love me and marry me or
Will I just be another fling on the history
Of your timeline, another booty call?
We skirt around the issues, play hide and seek
Play house with our assumptions
Instead of asking the questions
Are you someone I can grow with?
Are you the person I've been praying for?
And will you be able to sacrifice yourself so we can put god first?
And will you be able to listen to his voice when
He asks us to ignore our worldly thirst?
Are you my poetry?
Flesh of my flesh and bones of my bones
Will you love me, when loving is hard and
you don't even like me?
Will you love me, when loving is hard and

Charlynne Bryan

You don't even like me?
Will you love me, when loving is hard and
You don't even like me
We shy away from being that girl who asks that
Question...
Silently fall into familiar patterns
Instead of remembering that we
Were called to be greater ... Proverbs 31 women.

Letters to my soul

JIGSAW

I break into pieces over
And over and

No one is around to help me
Put myself back together. So I

Nurse my cracks and I
Apply adhesive the best

Way I can to keep myself from
Completely falling

Apart. And I am always breaking
And splintering and putting

Myself back into the jigsaw
I've become.

Charlynne Bryan

P A R I S

The bench stood
In the middle of the park
An unexpected sight
I stopped and stared
Because the fallen leaves
Resembled my discarded dreams
And all the colours I had painted them
Over the years
And their beauty
Weighed heavy on my chest
Had I known that I would be here
Again
I would have taken a different route
Yet I lingered here waiting
For the penny to drop
That he wasn't coming
And that when I boarded the plane tonight
I would never be coming pace.

Letters to my soul

STORM

I don't have dainty feet
Or delicate calves
My thighs would never
Be called petite
And my body, when you
See it is large and unhiding
I am thunder and hurricane
And the storm between
These thighs
Can bring salvation
Or destruction. I am
Force of nature
Bound by no certain rules
And fire and lightning storm
And avalanche
The greatest definition
Of war, the softest
Callings of peace.

Charlynne Bryan

FIRST LOVE

I learned to love with sarcasm on my tongue...
The bitter taste of criticism coating my taste buds
Love was an elusive bird flying out of reach
Creased eyebrows and eyes out of focus
On anything except mistakes
Love was a silent lip curled upward
A sneer in the corner waiting for reproach
Love was the food in the centre of the table
Where enemies waited to feast
I learned that love needed a show and
I needed to give one if I ever wanted approval
I learnt that there were always conditions
And so love wasn't unconditional
And I was the starving child
So I over-compensate
Make love the cup overflowing
Of which everyone must taste.
Put conditions on the feasting
While hoping no one notices
And so I walk blindly into anything
Resembling whole love,
Keeping my eyes closed so
I can't see the criticism while dishing
Out bitter fruits of my own
And so I stand in judgement,

Letters to my soul

Waiting
Waiting
Waiting
For love
To fail.

Charlynne Bryan

On some days I grapple
With standing in this frame
And owning the picture
Being taken. I
Feel uncomfortable
Creeping into my very
Bones and gripping
All that I could be, marring
It as illusion. still
This skin is home and hearth.
Still, this place called home
Follows me
And in this home
I find my rest.

Letters to my soul

Alone and afraid
She discovered the strength
She had within
She learnt that
Strength
Wasn't in the loud
Wasn't in the obvious
That strength
Was silence when
You felt only the need to scream.

Charlynne Bryan

Lean in

Letters to my soul

Charlynne Bryan

I will tell my daughters:
The world will come to devour you
To consume the very essence of your being
Men and women alike
Will try to strip you bare
You will be tested
At every opportunity
And people will determine your worth
According to the standards they have set
With no foundation
You must always remember who you are
Fight for who you want to be
And go against all the obstacles in
Place to stop you
Because the world is yours for the taking
The dragons are yours for the slaying
And you can, will, must rise to the top
Of every mountain you pace
And you can, will, must be unstoppable
In every encounter you face

Letters to my soul

SOUL TIES

I keep writing
Like my life depended on it
'Cause it does
See, every time I put pen to paper, I tether
My soul
To eternity
And I become
Immortal on these pages
As it enforces
A shield around
My aura
That saves me

Charlynne Bryan

I'M ALRIGHT

Exhausted
Doesn't quite cut it
When my very bones roll out of bed
Each morning craving the soothing release
Of waves lapping against my flesh
Wanting nothing more than to roll
Back into sweet oblivion
And welcome the dreams that had me wrapped
In their sweet embrace
I curse the day before it's even begun
Hook my thoughts into moments of longing
And saunter
Into some semblance of what I could have been
Had my days been ordered like I wanted them to be
When I greet the morning
Fresh faced, eyes shining
No one will know
That my heart has been left
On a shelf at home waiting
For my mother's call
Or my lover's touch
Or my nephew's laugh
When I step through door that lead
To nowhere, trading my soul for a place to lay my head

Letters to my soul

No one will guess that the excitement in my voice is a put on
And I am in a trance
Dancing in Some party in the sun
And I'm tired
Of lying through my teeth
Because this conversation is longer
Than we have time for.

Charlynne Bryan

E M P T Y

At the end of this life
I want to stand before my creator
And explain that I have lived
All the life that was in me to live
That I have loved
All the love that was in me to love
That I have laughed
All the laughter that was in me to laugh
That I have danced
Every dance that was in me to dance
That I have been
All that was in me to be
And that I have died empty
Because I gave the world
All of me that there ever was to give.

Letters to my soul

HOMEMADE

I am homemade
full bodied blues
Heavy textured silhouette
Rough around the edges
Like sweet honeycomb
I am homemade
Rustic charm
Stilted, blurred lines
Beneath strawberry, turbulent
Skies
Smoke hidden secrets
Dancing behind dusty lies
I am homemade
Dirty laundry piled high
Lacy veil shielding
Wondering eyes
Tense conversations
And lofty faked smiles
I am made with care
And a sprinkling of surprise
I am homemade.

Charlynne Bryan

H O M E

Home was never meant to be you
Should never have been
prison arms
Or steel shuttered heart
Or late night pleading
To feed your ravenous ego
Home was never meant to be
Wishful thinking
Or the deep craving for an epic love
I should never have searched for home
In the empty cavities of your chest
I should have continued, a rolling moss
In the opposite direction of you affection
Instead of allowing you to devour me
And searching for home in the
Aftermath of your avalanche
Home should never have been you
Home should never have been you
It should always have been me...

Letters to my soul

HOME IS WHERE THE ---- IS

Home is where the soul is
Where the stories spill out of every shelf
And jump out from behind every curtain
Reminding you of the peeping on your neighbour
Your mother did when you were younger and
You still do from time to time
For nostalgia's sake
Where the truth takes the form of anecdotes
Passed down through generations of folklore
That no one dared to question
And you don't dare either
Where your fears take root from the little things
You've seen behind closed doors
And couldn't run from
Where the love is suffocation - your brother's
Overprotective presence at every party
Warning the boys off,
Your parent's overbearing presence
At every gathering channelling
The embarrassment you can never run from,
Siblings huddling round a table set with
The little you've got,
Sharing everything but the skin
Covering your very bones.
Home is where you run away from,

Charlynne Bryan

Wanting escape, wanting greater horizons
Than your struggle
Home is where you return to,
To surrender to those that welcome you,
The prodigal, right back in.

Letters to my soul

H O M E

I've been careful to say welcome back
Instead of welcome home,
As though calling this place home is me
Cheating on the place that I left behind.
I've been careful to cry when I leave and
Feel sad even when I get back to the place I've built
As though my being happy to be back
Would be some sort of crime.
I've been careful to refer to this place as overseas
Citing 'back home' in all my talks
About the place where I was born
As though home isn't the place I carry with me
As though I don't wear home on my tongue
Like an intoxicated fool
As though home cannot be both
The place I left and the place I found.
I am careful to keep home separate from here
Instead of having to explain that home
Is here and there,
Both places I go back to.

Charlynne Bryan

H O M E

Home doesn't feel like home anymore
It's a seance with the past
Reaching out to the spirits of memories
Long since buried,
Harbouring a desperate need for familiarity,
Acceptance, closure.
With lights flickering in the distance of your mind
Home is the ghost that haunts you
Latches itself onto your conscious
Singing lullabies from yesteryear.
Home is the rose which stings with
The ferocity of nettle
Hinting at the sweetness of honeydew promises made
To call you back,
Back to what you knew,
What no longer exists.
Home doesn't feel like a haven anymore
It is the nest you remember through
Rose coloured spectacles
A lasting ache resting heavy in your chest
A longing for a life no longer there
Home is amnesia
A garden of forgotten feelings, places, people
Prickling the surface of composure
Home is a band snapped back into place

Letters to my soul

Displaced, disfigured, distorted
That burns your very core within
Clings to your soul and pulls you under
Home is an enigma
A place that's all too familiar
A place that's all too distant.

Charlynne Bryan

HOME

Home is nowhere now
Broken by the distance I crossed
When the ocean stretched between me
And my island, I struggle. To place
Myself here or there
Sometimes I feel like home no longer
Knows me. No longer wishes to welcome
The woman I have become because
It is still longing for the girl I
Used to be. Instead of this hollow
Feeling of longing that burns inside
My chest, I wish I could sing a return song
And run into her arms without her
Commenting on the change in my tongue
I'm trying. to put pieces of myself
Back together in ways that home
Recognises. In ways that home doesn't feel
The need to cast out but I remain
Conflicted as I fight myself and my
Ever growing places. When I look
Back I want to

Letters to my soul

Call home and be reconciled
Yet, whether she wants me back or not
I reach home and hold her always in
My heart instead of only in my mind.

Charlynne Bryan

HOMECOMING

I return here to this body I once shunned
To this home where disgust hung on the walls
Extending beyond the picture frames...
I return
Damaged
Hurting
Broken
Begging for forgiveness.

Letters to my soul

HOME

This body
Is my home
I refuse to allow
You to tell me
How to live in it.

Charlynne Bryan

THIS BODY

This body is sacred
It is not the watering hole for thirsty souls
Nor the feeding ground for hungry bellies
This body is holy
It is not the place where hollow promises come to die
Nor the graveyard of unsated desires
This body is worthy
It is not heavy tomes of unanswered questions
Nor late night musings on forbidden grounds
This body is temple
Resting place of the divine
The birthplace of miracles
This body is sanctuary
An altar for the offerings of truth
A haven overflowing with gifts of forgiveness
This body is shelter
Sanctum against the raging infernos
Harbour in every storm
This body is safety
Vessel of security and peace
Fountain overflowing with goodness and light
This body is inspiration
Reservoir of knowledge bursting at the seams
A symbol of unlimited supply
This body is sanctified

Letters to my soul

Embalmed with blessings from the gods
Cloaked in angelic reverence
This body is sacred
This body is home.

Charlynne Bryan

P R O P H E C Y (Black love story)

Never thought we'd make it here did you?
This space where we've dared to
Transcend the boundaries set before us
This space where knowledge, passion and power
Becomes spiritual, celestial, godly
This space where regal spews out
Of the cracks where normality tried to bury it
This common ground where palaces are ours
For the building upon the structures
We tore down to make space for them
Never thought we'd make it here did you?
Yet here we are
Born out of the need to connect, to intersect,
To reclaim
Connected to other drops becoming the ocean
And here we are
Standing on the promises of our ancestors
Walking through the eye of the storm
Gathering, on every side
The winds of change and becoming the hurricane
And aren't we magic
Divine deities cloaked in human form
Pulled from the ribs of mother earth herself
Fashioned into a holy nation,
Warriors

Letters to my soul

In this unholy war
Healers
In this time of calamity
Seers
In this haze of uncertainty
And aren't we magic
Conjuring dynasties from the very essence
Of the whispers of those who came before
Channelling that same alchemy into
Those who follow in our footsteps
And we hold knowledge in the palm of our hands
Pass the baton to those who stand with us...
Imbue truth into the armour of our words as we
Fight
To secure our salvation
For we foresee greatness on the horizons
A Multitude of generations
Standing before the throne we now rebuild
Hand in hand
For we foresee glory gleaming on the clouds
The silver lining on those dreams
We cultivated in deep dark trenches
And we see the fruits of our labour
Calling us to feast, to experience
The fullness of everything on offer
And we rise...
Gather those pieces of ourselves

Charlynne Bryan

Scattered across shores
That refuse to claim us
Link our arms together forming a collective
And we stand strong
Holding our devotion at the centre
Infusing everything we are and everything
We will become
With this purest form of love
And we are called back to the mother
To walk along the lines of our victory
And create home
To dance under the moonlight
And claim what is our own
To become what we need to be
To become everything we can foresee
To become what we already are.

Letters to my soul

I'M SORRY

I want to start with an apology
Because sometimes
I know I make you feel as though
I am comparing you to him
The one who broke my heart and
Nearly ruined my soul...
I can see it in your eyes when I mention
Anything about the past
How
You wish I could seal my mouth with wax
Lock my words in a prison of brass
And throw the key into an abyss.
How you want to tell me that words
Are the entrance to the pits of hell
When they are words wrapped around
Thoughts of him
How you would give anything to
Take the slate and wipe is so clean that
Even the slate itself disappeared and
All that was left was sand
In which I could scribble a new story.
I cannot talk about the here and now
Without bringing up the past
It is part of my history and it should be
History but

Charlynne Bryan

No matter how hard I try,
To keep it in the straitjacket of yesterday
It keeps knocking on the doors of Today,
Crawling out the window of this minute and
Bursting into the conversations of now.
And each time it arrives, it attacks you
Snakes its way off my tongue and looks
Scarily like a comparison
But I am not comparing you
To him or him
To you
There is no comparison
And if there was you'd be in first base
Heading confidently to first place
No fielders in sight to strike you out or
Slow you down, this
Would be a home run
Though it looks like a comparison.
Still how can I compare
Specks of dust to stars twinkling in the galaxy?
Or the warmth of the sun to a tiny spark
That never even grew to a glow?
You see I've been searching for a million light years,
My body floating about space trying to get grounded
Yearning for something
I've spun
In and out of orbit

Letters to my soul

Got caught up in the magnetic field of the
Many bodies I should never have been
Attracted to in the first place
Until you...
And you draw me in
Hold me close,
Keep me soaring into outer space
Let me be the explorer of the universe
I was meant to be
You ground me, anchor me to a love
That gives me wings and pushes me
Beyond the realms of this reality
So how can there be a comparison
When you are what I've been searching for
Since the beginning of time?
When you
With your soft love
And your fierce protection step into
My orbit and causes my comets to shift
Align to your intergalactic pull?
How can this be anything less than what it is?
A celebration of you
And the way you ensure that it's all about we
The way you dance into my memory and stay there,
A happy song that repeats its melody
In times when songbirds have all vanished.
I want to start with an apology

Charlynne Bryan

Because you deserve nothing less than the best of
What I can offer...
And there is no comparison
That will make his attributes turn you into
Anything less
Than who you are to me
You see
With us it's chemistry
We connected on deeper levels -
With poetry
And this poem is a lifeline
Beating slowly, pulsing through time
Whispering an, "I'm sorry" because
You never should have been here
In the first place.

Letters to my soul

SOMETIMES I OPEN MY MOUTH

Sometimes I open my mouth
And my mother comes out
Hijacking my conversation
She replaces it with her own
Laces my words with her criticisms
And colours my speech with her judgements
I can't seem to help when this happens
One minute I'm me
Living a life I've crafted
The next, my mother's tongue
Has taken over
Running a riot as it's unleashed
And I stand back amazed
At how uncanny the situation
Because though I am a million miles away
Somehow my mother still
Finds a way to speak through me.

Charlynne Bryan

And I cried myself to sleep last night
Because the ghosts still haunt me
And when I finally fell asleep I dreamt
About how you left me,
How I couldn't keep the light of hope
Flickering between us and about how you were
Always more concerned with leaving than loving me
And more tears fell as I stood by
And watched you walk away with pieces
Of me tucked into your pocket,
And beneath your collar,
And under your fingernails
And in your throat and I
Remembered the brokenness
That stretched out and cloaked me
I had belonged to you for so long
I didn't know what to do with me without you
I was lost. Still tears
Don't last forever
And once the wells within me closed up
I found that my internal compass
Had returned and I was ready
For new direction. I fought
Those demons that you left behind
And it seemed like I was fighting a losing battle
There were more wounds to heal
Than ointment to salve them

Letters to my soul

There were more doubts to fight off
Than there was confidence to strike them
And you had gotten under my skin
But that's the thing with battles
Soon everyone gets tired of fighting
Or someone wins and I am
Here winning this one
Because my joy came this morning
When I woke up and I was alone
You were no longer a ghost. I made it through
The night and now it is my moment to let
You go and to move on.

Charlynne Bryan

SWEET NOTHINGS

They mean nothing
These lyrics spewed out
From between your lips like confetti
Sweet in their delivery, they fall
Hollow calories becoming cavities
They stain the inside of my palate
Slide bitter down my throat
Where I am unable to digest them
Sweet nothings

Letters to my soul

NECTAR

I am sugar honey molasses
Sweet from the inside out
And outside right back in
I am syrup to your soul
Treat to your sweet tooth
Savour me
Dip your tongue
Between my petals
And find the bud of my
Ambrosia waiting to satisfy
Your every desire...
Have your fill
Quench your thirst
And bloom

Charlynne Bryan

I don't need you... I want you
I choose you
And isn't that a beautiful thing?
That I can decide
To walk away from you at any minute
But in each moment,
I choose you.

Letters to my soul

...IN OTHER WORDS I LOVE YOU

Life wouldn't mean the same thing
If you weren't here
You know me better
Than anyone I've ever encountered in my entire
Lifetime
I would cross the greatest chasm
Retrieve the biggest treasure
Fight the fiercest dragons
Face my deepest fears all for you
Yet you would never ask me to
And I rest in amazement at how
You challenge me to be a better me
With each passing moment
I can't, not in so many words
Ever say what you really mean to me
Words can't capture how my heart
Is filled to bursting with a kind of tender
Growing that has your name written on it
I pray for you on days when I forget to pray for me
Whisper incantations into the universe
Hoping that whatever kind of magic
Is required to keep you safe
Finds its way to do this bidding
You shine brighter than any galaxy

Charlynne Bryan

I have ever seen, sustain these hopes in me
With a mere hello and wherever I go
I hope to take you with me
To keep your place in my life
Reserved to the outer edges of space
Itself and back again
Nothing will destroy this tenderness you evoke in me
I want nothing but the best for you
I want nothing but the most for you
In other words, I love you.

Letters to my soul

S P A R K L E R

You can spark
You were infused with
Purpose. And the means to
Achieve that purpose. But
There is a catch, there always is.
You have to want to fulfil your purpose
So badly that not doing so
Would make it hard for you to even breathe.
Drawing that breath in a place less
Than your place of purpose would be
Like eating glass when a feast was
Laid out before you.
You must pursue your dream
Like it is the only thing you can see on your horizon.
That thing that causes your flame to
Begin its ignition, you have
To chase it with blind ambition,
Knowing that achieving it is
The one thing in life you must do
And if you catch that, you will spark
You will Set the trail ablaze
And you will become the fire.

Charlynne Bryan

EXPLORATION

We are an untapped resource
We are constantly discovering
Parts of ourselves we had no idea existed
We are not who we were yesterday
We are not who we will be tomorrow
We are constantly changing
We are constantly growing
We are constantly becoming
Who we truly are.

Letters to my soul

SUBMISSION

Your wife will not be a woman who looks like this
Breasts heaving with lust, legs bare
Calling out to be touched,
Neck upturned to the sun and body craving release
She will not stand uncovered on street
Corners shouting lewd slangs
She will not be seen fraternising
In places where women shouldn't go
She will not be seen
Your wife will not sound like this
Free will spewing from her lips
Words falling out of her mouth
Enticing men and women to allow
Their hearts to stray.
She will know her place and abide in it.
She will stand silent and await you
To put words into her mouth,
She will speak, only when spoken to
Lower her eyes to the ground in fear
Of offending you...
Not open her lips to say...
She will choke on her opposition
The words dying in her throat
Before finding their escape
She will be voiceless

Charlynne Bryan

Your wife will not be a woman who looks like me
Abrasion her weapon of choice, confidence her tone
She will comply.
Bend to your will, accept your every
Suggestion. She will be the definition of submission
Count her paces under breath to maintain
Her position
She will follow your direction
Your wife will not be a woman
Who's bold like this
Dare to be brazen and out of place
She will teach her daughters to
Resign their case.
But she will never be a woman who looks like me
Because me I do not know that look
And I, I cannot wear that face.

Letters to my soul

BIRDSONG

To be part of something greater is our birth-right
And all of nature knows it.
The birds sing their birdsong and
Add to the orchestra of the earth.
The flowers sway in dance,
The rivers provide rushing drum music
While the gazelles and the insects cha cha.
Everything plays its part in the great harmony of life.
It is only us humans who overthink our place.
We forget that we too are a part
Of maintaining the harmony.
We neglect the fact that we help to keep
The balance.
And we short-change ourselves
By getting into our own head and
Talking ourselves out of our importance
In this wonderful cycle called life.
Imagine what would happen
And how great it would be if we chose
To live in alignment.

Charlynne Bryan

CEASEFIRE

This body. Is not a war zone
And these words? Not grenades
There are no trip wires here
Waiting to detonate bombs that
Will consume, skin, sinew, bones
This war, created in my mind alone
From the opinions of others
Must stop. So, I have declared a cease fire
Held up a white flag and
Asked for a truce. Today we will walk
These battle grounds as allies.
My body and I. We will go through
The trenches hand in hand
As a form of celebration and
Kindness will reign here
Life breathed into grounds ruined by shrapnel words.
And flowers will grow here
In the fertile ground that replaces the ashes.
There has been enough fighting
To recover these stolen lands.
Enough verbal assassination of hopes and dreams
All because this body, larger than those on screens
Dared to survive another burst of bullets...
So this war ends now.
With soldiers deserting the cause

Letters to my soul

In a rebellion...So this war
Ends now. With renumeration paid
As a means of reconciliation. And this body
Will bloom into the poppy fields
Of remembrance to commemorate
A battle fought and won.

Charlynne Bryan

CONFESSION

I have decided to stand at the altar of reflection
And welcome in my soul
Strip myself before my demons
Allowing my fear to fall away
While I step up to the helm and take control
Been a victim of circumstance so long
I'm now hidden behind the plaster
Statuesque yet petrified until even
I become a believer.
Forgiveness stands close and ever tries
To take my hand
I bow my head in passing,
Knowing we are only lovers in the sand.
I will be here again after this feeling goes past
This reconciliation is fleeting,
Dancing on the wind, never meant to last...
And she can never hold me
Through all this anxiety that I bear
I've been my own worst enemy for so long
I realise, it's myself that I fear.
But it can't end here...
So I look failure in the eyes,
Peel back the stories, confront the lies
If I'm going out like this
I will be forthcoming in my last wishes,

Letters to my soul

Direct in my goodbyes.
No standing here in resignation
I must be the bold executor of my own direction.
And when I confront who I am
It will be the perfect execution
Because if I cannot be bound to my soul
There will be no other soul binding
I will wait on the edge of this precipice
And take care of my own unwinding
And I won't allow the demons I've been running from
To outrun me by any means
This confrontation has been a long time coming,
Time to own up to my sins.

Charlynne Bryan

RADIANT

This glow is godly
It's the light of the divine
Shining in me that places me
In these places of majesty
And I bring daylight to the darkness
Walking tall, I rise up and shine the way
Before me so that all I touch exudes beauty
And I am the cloud's silver lining
The never-ending burst of lightening
That illuminates the sky....
And you never have to worry
That you can't see me, because:
Even in the absence of sunlight
I am the sunshine.

Letters to my soul

R I S E

She came out fighting
Her nails turned into claws
To help her climbing
And she transformed
From a hummingbird
Into an Eagle
All to escape from you
Now she's no longer running
As she took to the skies
Her head held high,
She realised she was winning
For those trials that almost made her die
Hadn't been her undoing
Instead she was strengthened
Forged through these mines
A diamond in the making
And she was shining
Reigning on high
The world was hers for the taking.

Charlynne Bryan

VENUS

She is a wildflower
Growing in the wilderness
She is beautiful and strong
She is Radiant and alluring
But never forget
That her roots need
Watering too.

Letters to my soul

CLARITY

The maze in my head has disappeared and I can see the path before me clearly. There is no chatter in fifty different languages confusing me. I step forward and proceed – sure in my steps, secure in my ability to make those decisions that matter. Is this what knowing feels like? This clearing of the haze. This walking through the fog with improved sight? It amazes me that this place even exists. Yet here I am. Walking - though not blindly.

Charlynne Bryan

Break free

Letters to my soul

Charlynne Bryan

CATER

She is fighting to come out
Can't you see?
The little girl
You used to be
Desperate to have
Her day in the sun
Crying out
For some old fashion fun

She wants to reconnect
To the things that made her laugh
She wants you to take her
Down the less trodden path
Your inner child
Just wants to explore
She is calling out to you
What are you waiting for?

Cater to her simple pleasures
Her every whim
Answer that pressing need
From deep within
Give her the chance to run and play
Let her out in the sun today!

Letters to my soul

LAUNDRY

I need to wash you off my bed sheets
I can still smell your deceit
All those lies you fed me to keep me sweet
Clinging to the fabric
Long after you are gone
And I haven't quite brought myself to get rid of you
Yet
Your essence still intoxicating
Drawing me in to that false sense of security
You are the wolf in sheep's clothing
And the boy who cried wolf wrapped into one
And I keep falling into your traps
'Cause you remember don't you
How I moan out your name when I am wriggling
Beneath you
How the scratches on your skin
That remain for weeks after
Are you marking your perimeter
And I can never quite understand how
I'm the one doing the marking
yet it is you doing all the benefiting
Cause when we're here you say all those things I need
To hear
To keep me falling
Falling into you

Charlynne Bryan

The bottomless pit
Falling into you, the abyss
And there are no sides to cling on to
I can't seem to hold on to you
So instead I inhale the smoke, screens and mirrors
That you have always been
And choke on the fumes I taste on your tongue
You deceive me
Spin sugar sweet honey into the web
That traps me
Dangle promises of tomorrow like carrots on a string
And like the ass I've always been with you
I'm the one doing the chasing
How could I forget that it was I who let you into this
Holy place
How could I forget that you are here by invitation
How could I forget that this is my sanctuary
And you have always been
Just visiting
How could I forget?
So I strip my bed off its bedding
While I strip my heart off its bleeding
Wash the remnants of you off my skin
Trying to make a clean break from you
I do my dirty laundry
And expunge the ghosts of you I know will always
Haunt me

Letters to my soul

When I sleep tonight
Maybe I won't dream of you
Because at least, you will no longer be lingering
On my bedsheets
The way you still linger on my mind.

Charlynne Bryan

TAILOR-MADE

Adjust your thinking
So that it serves you instead
Of destroying the purpose in your soul
Adjust your mindset
So that you can believe in the power
You possess to reach your goal
Adjust your crown
From where it started to slip off,
Remind yourself that you are queen
Adjust your view,
Stop trying to find jewels in the distance,
Instead look within
Adjust your senses
So, they tune in to the truth and
Remind you to let yourself shine through
Adjust everything
That needs to be adjusted
For you to truly be you!

Letters to my soul

ARTIST

When words fail me I turn to paints
Pour out my feelings from
Tubes of acrylics and move them around
With my brushes
I mix the yellow greens of my envy
With the reds of my anger in hopes
The oranges they create will bring forth fire
Some days I am calm blues and
Cool hues of turquoise
Waiting patiently on the shoreline
For those dreams I casted into the oceans
Some days I turn my palette over to
The romance of tinted rose and
Dip my wishes in gold
And then there are other days still
Where my charcoal existence seeps into the
Spotlight, tingeing
Almost everything with shadows
Of doubt, and regret and shame
And I have to tint my thinking
With a little chartreuse to try and
Let the light back in

Charlynne Bryan

But on most days, though words fail me
I still remember that I am the canvas
Working with all the colours of the rainbow.

Letters to my soul

You know that chance you've been meaning to take?
Take it
Dance under the skylight like you'd planned
Do the marathon or not
Walk down to that lake
Strip off your clothes and jump in
Climb that mountain
Send that message
Go on that date
Eat. The. Damn. Chocolate.
Stop living your life trying
To please everyone and their mother
Your life belongs to you and you alone
In the end, none of those people you were trying
To please will be there with you,
Regretting the things you didn't do
Your regrets will be yours alone
So live your life for you today.

Charlynne Bryan

NUDE

I go naked
Bare my soul
Spiritually
Physically
Reduce barriers
That's been constricting me
And I stand before
God
In this nudity
Hoping that he sees
Me
Unencumbered by
The expectations
Of this dimension
I expose my inner
Being
Clinging
Grasping
Hoping
That I am
Who he called me
To be
Despite all
The mediocrity.

Letters to my soul

DECLARATION

Chaos tries to sink me under
Until I feel like I'm drowning in it
With nowhere to turn for help
No one to confide in to ease my mind
And I sink
Further into all the ways I am not good enough
Until
A moment of clarity
And I stop
Dust the debris off of me
And I remember
I've made it through worse than this before
This. Too. Shall. Pass.

Charlynne Bryan

Let's talk about us
Not the us we want to be or imagine
But the us that we actually are
Not the illusion –
The fabricated mirage created
By smoke and mirrors
But the reality
The flesh, the blood
The truth and the lies

Letters to my soul

AFFIRMATION

I let go of the idea that you belong to me
As I hold this space for us to commune.
I free you to be who you need to be outside of my
Conditions.
I free you to be you as you were meant to be.
I am grateful for the here and now.
The fullness we share when we are together,
The love that connects us back to who we were
From the moment of our conception.
I choose to accept my part in this universe we
Have become.
To give my all for us to be one.
I am ready for the mystic explosion that will ensue.
The landing, into the softest part of our destiny.
I deserve this freedom of self and expression,
The lack of judgement to allow myself to flourish,
To grow into my soul space.
I am learning to be the vessel
Through which life flows. The lyric
That completes the song and the song all at once.
To let go of the hurt and pain of yesterday
As I wake up into my power.
I am powerful.

Charlynne Bryan

I am faithful in my quest to self-love.
Being me and free is my divine right
And I am open to receiving it now.

Letters to my soul

VOICE 'FULL'

My voice
Scares you
Words that I only use
To claim my place
In a world where
I've been told that
My voice isn't important
You react
As though my voice
Is a war
Regardless of what I say
Try to shut me down,
Cut me off
Yet I will
Not be silenced
As long as I have words
I will speak.

Charlynne Bryan

I LOOK FOR POEMS IN EVERYTHING

I look for poems amidst the petals
Of flowers long before they begin to bud
Dig through the earth beneath my feet
And find lyrics written in the soil
Savour the wind on my tastebuds
Tingling with the flavour of a verse
Marinated for a moment with the hues of seasons
Poems call out to me from book pages and
Musical notes
From forbidding gates and no trespassing signs
I look for poems in the sighs of lovers
And the knuckles of fighters
I search in between the cracks of hope
And inside the bubbles of despair
I look for poems everywhere
And sometimes poems flit
Into my consciousness
When I'm not even looking
Splice through all the fibres of me
And take over my entire being
And sometimes they spill out in the perspiration
On my skin
Seep out of my eyes, ears and nose

Letters to my soul

And they find me willing and waiting
Because I look for poems in everything
And often I find, poems are looking for me too.

Charlynne Bryan

I'm learning to take my disappointment
And hide it beneath my tongue
I'm learning that you don't owe me
An explanation
And I
Owe it to myself
To walk away from your toxic.

Letters to my soul

CLIMAX

Reading us back
It's like poetry in motion
The hints of your caress on my skin
Heightening sweet sensations
Just the idea of you and me
And our coming fusion
Guarantees I'm there,
Ready for the
Impending explosion
And I unfurl before you
As you touch me there and
Grant me the permission
To release the nectar
On the brink of spilling over
And we ride together
Soar with each other
...total surrender
Perfect execution...

Charlynne Bryan

SOULMATE

My soul cries out
Wanting nothing more than to hold you
I stand here and bare myself
Pour out my all into your atmosphere
Daring you to hold me, contain the entity that I am
You rise to the challenge
I am woman, your woman
I birth the energy you share with me
Release the essence of my spirit into our creation
You give, I take, you take, I give
Powers combined, we face the hurricanes of life
Stand together side by side
And perfect this dance of communicated harmony
My centre connected to yours and you to me
Symmetry, perfectly.

Letters to my soul

LOVE HANDLES

Love handles my love handles well
Says he likes fat girls but
Don't say it like that, he calls me curvy instead
Kisses every inch of my mind with his lyrical verses
Before he ever touches my body
Sings praises about my attitude, my flair, my style
Makes me believe it when he says he loves me.
Love caresses my skin in a simple form of worship
Bows down before the temple of my womanhood
And lays offerings at the apex of my thighs
Calls me queen as a means of exultation,
Yeah, love raises me up with those natural highs.
Love awakens desires when our souls
Touch, connect, intertwine
Reassures me I have nothing to fear,
In the grander scheme of things, he's always been
Mine
Love holds on longer than needed,
Stays longer than necessary
Loves me better than ever
Then leaves me higher than I've ever been.
But
Love
Still
Leaves.

Charlynne Bryan

He likes girls that look like me but sound different
Barbed wire shoved around their tongues to guard
An arsenal
Thoughts barricaded on the inside of the safe zone
Words electrocuted way before the firing line
He likes girls that dress like me but act different
Steps packed into neat little squares within the lines
Knees tucked in, legs folded under,
Clasped shut until they resemble proper
Hips smoothed over off rhythm, off time
He likes girls that taste like me
But dream different
Role playing within an inch of sanity
As they hide behind the disguise they
Paint to cover the scars his words created
When he took the time
To voice his displeasure at their true nature
He likes girls that are seen and not heard
That bow their head in servitude, accepting his lead
But these girls lack flavour
And authenticity
That's why he keeps searching for me
Between the parameters
Of all the girls he finds
Yet comes up lacking each time.

Letters to my soul

FAMILIAR STRANGERS

And I hate this,
The way we talk like we ain't ever been familiar
And the words fall from our lips like we strangers.
And I hate this,
How formal we've become sitting at arm's length
As though we ain't mapped the very contours
Of each other's bodies
And committed it to memory.
As if we cannot navigate each other's expanse of
Skin
Blind folded and still pinpoint
Our hearts beating in unison.
And I hate how we are strangers,
Forlorn lovers torn apart,
Anchored within reach yet worlds apart
Our love fading into a background
Foreign and forbidden
And I hate
How we're meant to be together
But timing leaves us
Alone

Charlynne Bryan

SAFETY SIGNS

Be careful
To not fall into the trap of dependency
To not feel like you need their voice
To make everything ok
Be careful
To not feel like they are your happiness
And when they are gone
Your world is no longer alright
Be careful to not think that lonely
Means you are missing someone
Because having people doesn't
Send loneliness packing
Be careful to remember
That you existed
Before the loving and were
Whole
That you will exist again even after
The loving and will still be
Whole
Be careful to not diminish your power
To pieces that you hide behind
The clutter in your mind
Be careful of accepting praise
To confirm you
Even when sometimes you may feel

Letters to my soul

Like you need confirmation.
Be careful to remind yourself
That you are the sunshine
Be careful to remind yourself
That you are the treasure
Be careful to remind yourself
That you are the prize

Charlynne Bryan

TIME LAPSE

They say time is a healer
Of all wounds and an easer of pain.
Let enough time pass on something and soon
You will see it fade into the insignificance that it is
The hurt gets smaller until it almost doesn't
Hurt at all.
They say that time will make you question
Everything, confront everything
Sit you down at the table of remembrance
And shove memories into your mouth
Turning you into a glutton for yesterday
While starving you of that reality.
They say time takes care of it all
Crusts over the skin on
The scab that once was your love
Washes over the sand where
Your disappointment left its imprint...
Lights it up. Crashes. Burns
They say give it time
But time, you see time
Is a shut down of my pride
A reminder that I shouldn't have held on so long
Or given in so quickly
It is the essence of my failure

Letters to my soul

Wrapped tightly around my throat into the noose
That will strangle me
The final nail in the cross used to hang
My hopes and the coffin used to bury
My dreams at the same time.
Time is the enemy
The robber of memory

Charlynne Bryan

This woman that I am
Is not the woman that I was
Or the woman that I thought I'd be
Although this woman I am still is me,
She is a battle between
Wallflower and wild rose
Shoots pushing through soil
After she's been buried
She is the thin line between
Yesterday and today
Skirting the edges of
Stories, seeking truth
She is the reasoning between
The fabrication and the reality
Peeling back the layers of boundaries
Laid down by them who no one knows
This woman that I am
Is a mark against the shadow I once was
A gentle uprising
A subtle protest

Letters to my soul

TO THE MOON AND BACK

When I say I love you to the moon and back
What I mean is:
The moon will die out a thousand times
Before my love for you would ever run out.
What I mean is:
The love in my chest is so large and so heavy
That running to the moon is the only way
I know to make it weightless so I can get some relief
What I mean is:
I have searched the moon a million times over
To see if there is a bigger love, a truer love
And have not found a more intense love,
Leading me to run back to you – full.
What I mean is:
If the moon didn't exist
The galaxy would have to carve a path
Out of meteoric dust, flung far into the darkest
Reaches of the universe to make space for my love
Arching out and back again.
When I say I love you to the moon and back
I mean I love you
No holds barred...
No emotion spared,
From the top to the bottom and back again.

Charlynne Bryan

GILDED

Been on the brink of a breakthrough for so long
I sort of forgot that it was I wielding the tools to
Make changes.
Sort of forgot that there could be no breakthrough
Without the breaking.
Sort of forgot that I could get through once I was
Broken
Sort of became stuck
On the brink... neither here nor there
Waiting
When all along I was the powerhouse of a revolution
The gold placed in the cracks to revive the broken.
I was waiting for a solution that wasn't coming
'Cause I was the solution
And always had been in the making.

Letters to my soul

DEFINITION

And if
You ever start to doubt
Who you are
Close your eyes and listen.
To the beat of your heart
To the rush of your blood
Flowing in your veins
To your breath as it goes in
Through your nose and fill up your
Lungs.
Uncurl your fist and feel
The raise of skin beneath your
Fingertips.
The vibration of your heartbeat.
The rise and fall of your
Chest as you inhale, exhale.
The warmth that is you.
The strength that is you.
And if
You ever start to doubt
Who you are
Close your mind off from
Your doubts and remind yourself
You are human, superhuman.

Charlynne Bryan

And she knew fierce came through
Her flaws
And she knew strength was the story
Of each scar
And she knew confidence was the smile
In her eyes that always made it
To her lips.
And she knew that she was power
Radiating energy beyond what her eyes
Could see.
And she knew that all the ideals she
Had once struggled with could never
Hold up to her truth, could never
Stand the test of time
And she knew beauty was her soul,
The kindness she showed to everyone
The love she gave freely expecting nothing
In return
The genuine voice of her cares for those
In need.
And she knew who she was came through
Her standing, came through her living,
Came through her being.

Letters to my soul

BE YOU

Find you in the cracks they used to hide you
Alive, growing, blooming, thriving
Know you in the entirety that you exist
Whole, worthy, valid, enough
See you through the eyes of the gods
Magnificent, pure, special, valuable
Love you despite being human and flawed
Precious, unconditional, deep, strong
Be you as you were ordained to be
Powerful, purposeful, confident, right
Respect you as you give thanks to creation
For you are beautiful, spectacular, fine.

Find you among the starlight
Shining brightly, glowing out
Know you in good times and adversity
Understanding your strength, gentle and precise
See you rise above the music and
Become the melody, harmoniously sung
Love you with every bit of your being
So you can teach others how to love you
Be you with no apologies
Live in your truth, live your truth

Charlynne Bryan

Respect you and give you all you deserve
So you won't experience lack and go
Searching for fullness in empty people.

Letters to my soul

M I N E

I've had to come back to myself
To claim the pieces of me I had given away
To take hold of my jigsaw shards
And match them back together again
I've had to welcome back the she that
She'd been before the world interfered
Or at least make space for the her that she
Could be once the negative energy got cleared
She, me had been a mirage in the
Distance through the desert I've called life
Absent. For most parts in fragments and
Void of authenticity as I've put on the masks
Created by me to appease everyone in society
But in times of dire need I've learnt that
No one is there to hold me the way I
Wrap my arms around myself and
Console her. That I've been my greatest cheerleader
And so I've had to come back to the me I
Have always been, unlearn some of the things
I'd seen and accept that when it came
To belonging – I belonged to me.

Charlynne Bryan

SOUL SISTERS

They held this space for me
Welcomed me into a circle of trust
Where the links were so secure, I knew
They would never be broken
And they allowed me
To pour out my fears into the well
In the centre
One by one I emptied them
Cleared out my vessel until there were
No more left. And they held me
As I faced the skeletons in my closet
That I had hidden there a long time ago
And they heard me
Beneath the noise of the world outside
They heard the silent plea I couldn't
Speak out loud
And they saw me
Under all the layers I had been hiding beneath
In the purity and realness of who I was
And they poured into me
Love to replace the hurt that once filled me
Love to coat the walls where the bullets had pierced
Love to fill the cracks and the scars the world had
Subjected me to
Love to combat the self – doubt

Letters to my soul

Love to battle the self – loathing
And they offered
A chance to exist, stripped of all the conditions
A place to scream out at the heavens for
All the pieces of me that had been taken without my
Consent
And they helped me
To understand
To accept
To begin where I was
To take one step
To focus only on one moment at a time
To heal
To plant myself in new soil
To be sunned
To grow
To thrive.

Charlynne Bryan

And ain't it beautiful?
When you stand in the fullness that is you
And let go...
Of all the things you've been holding on
To that never brought you joy
And ain't it marvellous?
When you accept that letting go
Doesn't mean losing
That giving it all up doesn't mean
You remain empty
That choosing to walk away
Doesn't mean you gon' be lonely
And ain't it wonderful?
When you realise that saying goodbye
Means you've accepted your value
And finally understood your worth
Means that instead of begging for
Friendship and love
You've decided to put you first
And ain't that self-love thing amazing?
That you gonna nurture and cherish
The bits of you that you've been ignoring
That taking care of you in the
Places you were hurting
Leads to your healing
And growing
And thriving

Letters to my soul

And ain't it just magical?
When you know without a doubt
That everything gon' be ok.

Charlynne Bryan

STUMBLING OVER CHAOS

I stumbled over chaos to get here
Trudged through exploding hopes,
Lost dreams and forgotten promises
Palms raw, knees bruised
From where I had to push myself
Up from the ground – I still made it
Pride wounded; expectations shattered
In the process of refining
Me into this – I am still here
The fighter who stands back up,
Dusts the splinters of broken glass off
And keeps going
I stumbled over chaos
Befriended the disorder trying to
Laugh in my face
Courted the danger threatening to destroy me
Danced with disharmony at the place
Where my soul cried out
I stumbled, fell to my knees
Remembered I was in the perfect position
To call out to the deities. Gathered strength
To get back up to my feet
I stumbled, mumbled, fumbled through –
Still here I am.

Letters to my soul

HERE

Here I call myself to be accountable
To answer for all the mistakes I have made
That were deliberate
Here I whisper to me that I no longer
Have to hide from the woman I am
Nor shrink from the woman I can become
Here I take my hand and lead me
Into my God space, tell me that I am enough
That I have always been the salt of the earth
Conscious bodied and full flavour I tell me
That though the world has taken chips
Off me, I am not broken. Never broken
Here I urge me to stand up, stand tall
Stand royal. To claim the passage
Into my divine. Here I call myself
To be free.

Charlynne Bryan

H A I R

I change my hair often
I do it to keep me decent
To make sure my style is recent
To ensure I don't get lost behind its follicles
Hair has a defining power see
This afro, kinky, curly top
Exclaims more about me when I
Walk into a room than my voice
Can ever say
People place me into brackets based
On how I wear it and these strands
Moulded into something special by
These blessed hands prove that
There is so much more to who I am
Than just this static existence
'Cause there is magic in how it stands
These strands – power in how
They define gravity – power
In how their story places me
Amidst a rich and colourful history
Power in the understanding that it is nothing
But the power I give to it. So I change
My hair to make the statement I need
And I dare you to take notice.

Letters to my soul

MY SISTER'S KEEPER

I am my sister's keeper here in this world
Of fake fame
Until my sister rises beside me and takes her place
In the spotlight.
I am my sister's keeper at the dinner table
Until my sister is offered
The bigger plate
I am my sister's keeper on the dance floor
Until my sister is approached and asked to dance
Then I throw shade trying to dim her light
Then I try to convince her
That the food is poisoned
Then I tell her she has no rhythm
Why can't I keep being my sister's keeper
When she is growing? Keep being my sister's
Keeper when she is glowing? Why does my
Envy not stay hidden? Why can't I
Really be my sister's keeper?

Charlynne Bryan

Let the light in
To touch all those
Places where darkness
Thought it came to
Stay.

Letters to my soul

SEASONS

And life is a season of change
Twists and turns through
Countless obstacles set to
Put you on a trajectory
For greatness if you overcome
Them or failure if you don't
You can never wind the clock
Back on time spent learning
The lessons you need to learn
Before your days here are over
But you can always continue from where
You are and start a new adventure.
Taking what you need so you
Can become epic and extraordinary
And you can achieve your every
Purpose because whether
You know it or not, there's greatness
In you that sets you apart and is waiting
For your explosion.

Charlynne Bryan

The world will try to tell you
That you are less than who you are
It is up to you to remind yourself
Of your 'moreness'
You are more amazing
More spectacular
More capable
More you
Than the world gives you credit for.
          Oh come on, you are magic!

Letters to my soul

HAPPY PLACE

It is here I find my peace
At the water's edge, waves
Lapping my ankles.
Here in the azure blue beneath
The blazing sun, here
Silhouetted against the cobalt
Sky, I find me...
Here no judgement exists about
My tongue and how it utters
Words that are foreign and
Forbidden. There is no critic here
No nose turned up at my body – too
Large, too heavy.
Here on this stretch of Caribbean
Beach I become like the palm trees
That offer respite to my melanin.
Here I am tall, magnificent, beautiful.
Here I reign supreme as years of
Inhibitions wash away with each
Wave that crashes against the shore.
Here I am reminded that I am
Regal too.

Charlynne Bryan

What a wonderful feeling it is
When you decide to set yourself
      Free
And live beyond all the
      Boundaries
That ever existed.

Letters to my soul

WITCHCRAFT

There is soft magic in the air
That whips all things into shape
And whispers to the broken soul
In all of us to heal
To come back from beyond the graves
And walk again among those
In the land of the living.

Charlynne Bryan

I ran away once
Took bits of myself
And packed them into neat
Little boxes that I labelled carefully
With the words 'no longer here'
There was a broken heart
That was too fragile to touch
And shattered expectations that
Were waiting to be swept up into
Corners where they could become cobwebs
And I kept running –
Running toward a new kind of meaning
Toward a hope that I could make it
Despite leaving pieces of myself behind
But I couldn't take it any longer
Living as a shell
So now, I'm running back to me.

Letters to my soul

Sister you've been on my mind
And I've been wondering how I can
Stand by you and celebrate the woman
You are, the journey you've been on
I've been keeping an eye on you,
Praying for you, lifting you up to the heavens
And asking for abundance to flow through for you
I've got news for you. Your breakthrough
Is on its way. God is shining his light on you
And bringing you to your place of glory.
You are powerful sis. Trust me your
Time is here. You are powerful sis
You are able, capable, valid
Remember your name is queen
Remember you were called to greatness
Even when you cannot see it.
You are the uprising sister
The answer to the question you have
Always been asking. It's been you sis
It's always been you
And I want you to know sis that
You shine.
I'm here for you. I'm here with you.
I celebrate you and I am always
Thinking about you.

Charlynne Bryan

MUSE

And she, had the stars within her shining
Forming galaxies of possibilities
That were her through and through.
And she was the heavens itself
The most celestial of bodies orbiting life
Bringing forth the very creation she foresaw
And in her palms was the power of the cosmos
Linking interstellar twinkles
Into a sparkling web of discovery and invention
And she, spewed inspiration from her very pores
Caused the glow and tides of the moon
Enabled the solar flares of the sun
Permitted the birthing of planets to adorn her sky
And
She was the universe itself
Manifestation of the prophecy between her and
Nature
Her form was divine
Her intellect supreme
And she was all there ever was and ever could be
The genesis and the apocalypse
The origin and the conclusion
She was the surge of energy pulsing
Through the roots of civilisation
Quite simply, she was art.

Letters to my soul

SUGAR RUSH

If wishes were horses...
So I've stopped wishing
That unicorns will fall
Out of the sky into my
Sphere. Instead I have begun
Crafting the cotton candy kisses
That will become my sugar rush
And spur me on...

Charlynne Bryan

You must remember to be grateful
For all the times you made it and all the times
You didn't
You must remember to look up to the sky and
Thank the gods for the victories and the near
Misses.
You must offer up the prayers of thanksgiving
For whatever and whoever comes into your life
Because they are there to bless you with lessons
And your learning is imperative to your growing.
So take your time to send your love through the
Ether...
When you give the love that spurts from your
Chest it forms a film that envelopes the world
In light.
Keep going, keep being, keep loving, keep
Knowing that you are the firework and you are
Required to be here as we live and we breathe
And as we rise up... tonight, we celebrate.

Letters to my soul

Let's stop this toxic way of living
This blame game and waiting
For reconciliation
From the other person
When we are the ones who
Started the argument
Let's normalise saying sorry for
The things we did that were wrong
Own up to our mistakes
And allow peace to flow
Let's talk about it
Work through it
Work at it
Together

Charlynne Bryan

MORNING MUSINGS

You don't inspire me to write poetry
The way the others did.
I don't find verses somersaulting around my
Brain waiting to burst from my pen
I don't have metaphors dancing on my tongue
About how you love me
Ours is not a love of flowery language and
Tomes hidden in sunsets or sunrises
With you, I live poetry
Feel the shivers run up my spine
When you touch me
Know that the laughter we share is more real
Than those describes through sonnets.
With you poetry is:
Every ordinary conversation
Every good morning kiss
Every late-night text to wish me goodnight
With you, I don't need fancy flourishes
Instead, I jump into reality and stop hiding
Behind my pen...

Letters to my soul

LETTERS TO MY SOUL

Today is the day to *fall back*

To stop telling yourself the lies
That you have been drip fed
For generations

Today is the day to *lean in*

To embrace the beauty
Of this life and to smile freely
To walk into the peace you are entitled to

Today is the day to *break free*

To jump into yourself
And live the life you were
Put on this Earth to live

Printed in Great Britain
by Amazon